Anguilla Island
Travel Guide 2023

Traveler's GeoData Handbook

Destiny Brian

Table of Contents

Water sports and recreational activities snorkeling, sailing, etc.
Cultural and historical landmarks to visit museums, art galleries, etc.
Nature reserves and hiking trails for outdoor enthusiasts
Local festivals and events worth experiencing for a travel guide to Anguilla as a tourist

Chapter Four: Dining and Nightlife in Anguilla
Anguilla's culinary scene and local specialties
Recommendations for fine dining restaurants and local eateries
Information on beach bars, lounges, and nightlife hotspots

Chapter Five: Outdoor Activities in Anguilla
Watersports opportunities kayaking, paddleboarding, etc.
Sailing and boat excursions around the island
Golf courses and tennis facilities
Yoga retreats and wellness centers

Chapter Six: Shopping and Souvenirs in Anguilla

Introduction

Welcome to the paradise island of Anguilla, a hidden gem nestled in the Caribbean Sea. With its pristine beaches, crystal-clear turquoise waters, and warm hospitality, Anguilla is the perfect destination for travelers seeking a tranquil and luxurious getaway.

Situated in the Eastern Caribbean, Anguilla is a small island measuring only 16 miles long and 3 miles wide. Despite its small size, this British Overseas Territory boasts an abundance of natural beauty and cultural richness that will captivate your senses.

As you step foot on the powdery white sands that stretch for miles along the coastline, you'll be greeted by the gentle sound of the waves and a refreshing ocean breeze. Anguilla is renowned for its stunning beaches, each offering a unique experience. From the popular Shoal Bay East, with its vibrant beach bars and water sports activities, to the secluded Maundays Bay, where you can unwind in peace and serenity, there is a beach to suit every mood.

Beyond its breathtaking beaches, Anguilla's charm lies in its vibrant culture and welcoming locals. The rich history of the Island is reflected in its engineering, music, and cuisine. Take a stroll through the charming capital, The Valley, and admire the colorful colonial-style buildings. Immerse yourself in the island's cultural heritage at the Heritage Collection Museum, where you can learn about Anguilla's past through artifacts and exhibits.

No visit to Anguilla would be complete without indulging in its world-class culinary scene. The island is renowned for its diverse dining options, ranging from beachfront barbecues to fine dining establishments. Sample the local delicacies such as grilled lobster, conch fritters, and johnnycakes, or savor international flavors crafted by talented chefs from around the world.

For those seeking adventure, Anguilla offers an array of activities to satisfy your adventurous spirit. Explore the underwater wonders of the island through snorkeling or scuba diving, where you'll encounter vibrant coral reefs and a kaleidoscope of tropical fish. Embark on a boat tour to the neighboring uninhabited islands, such as Prickly Pear Cay or Sandy Island, and discover secluded coves and hidden treasures.

When it comes to accommodations, Anguilla offers a range of luxurious resorts, boutique hotels, and private villas that cater to every traveler's needs. Whether you prefer a beachfront retreat, a hillside hideaway with panoramic views, or a secluded villa for ultimate privacy, you'll find your perfect haven on this enchanting island.

With its idyllic beaches, rich culture, and warm hospitality, Anguilla promises an unforgettable experience for every traveler. So pack your bags, leave your worries behind, and embark on a journey to this Caribbean paradise. Welcome to Anguilla, where relaxation and adventure await you at every turn.

Overview

Anguilla is widely known as a breathtaking gem nestled in the cerulean waters of the Caribbean Sea. This travel guide is your passport to an unforgettable journey through this paradise island, where pristine beaches, vibrant culture, and exquisite cuisine await you.

Getting There: You can reach Anguilla by air or sea. The closest international airport is Clayton J. Lloyd International Airport (AXA), with connections from various major cities.

Alternatively, take a ferry from nearby islands like St. Maarten.

Best Time to Visit: Anguilla boasts a tropical climate year-round, but the peak tourist season is from December to April, when the weather is most pleasant. The off-season from May to November offers lower prices and fewer crowds, though it's important to note that hurricane season falls within this period.

Accommodation: Choose from a range of luxurious resorts, boutique hotels, and charming villas. From beachfront bungalows to hillside retreats, Anguilla has accommodation options to suit every preference and budget.

Top Attractions: Shoal Bay: One of the Caribbean's most beautiful beaches, with powdery white sand and calm turquoise waters.

The Valley: Explore the island's capital, home to historic sites, local markets, and galleries that showcase Anguilla's art scene.

Sandy Island: A tiny islet perfect for snorkeling, picnics, and basking in the sun.

Prickly Pear Cays: Unspoiled paradise offering opportunities for snorkeling, swimming, and lounging on pristine shores.

Dolphin Discovery: Interact with dolphins in a natural lagoon, creating lifelong memories.
Cultural Experiences:

Carnival: If you're visiting in August, join the lively festivities of Anguilla's carnival, complete with colorful parades, music, and local cuisine.

Cuisines and Beach Bars: Savor the island's diverse culinary scene, ranging from gourmet restaurants to beachside shacks serving up fresh seafood and traditional dishes.

Art Galleries: Engage with Anguilla's artistic spirit by visiting local galleries that showcase paintings, sculptures, and crafts by talented local artists.

Outdoor Activities:

Watersports: Engage in snorkeling, diving, paddleboarding, and kayaking in the crystal-clear waters.

Boat Tours: Embark on catamaran cruises, sunset sails, or private yacht charters to explore the coastline and neighboring cays.

Hiking and Biking: Discover Anguilla's natural beauty by hiking along scenic trails or biking through picturesque landscapes.

Practical Tips:

Currency: The Eastern Caribbean Dollar (XCD) is the official currency, but US dollars are widely accepted.

Language: English is the official language.
Health and Safety: Pack sunscreen, insect repellent, and any necessary medications. Tap water is safe to drink.

Respect Local Customs: Anguillan culture is warm and friendly; it's customary to greet locals with a friendly "Good day!"

Transportation: Taxis are the most common mode of transportation; car rentals are also available for those who wish to explore independently.

Anguilla promises an idyllic escape, where turquoise waters, pristine beaches, and vibrant culture merge into an unforgettable travel experience. Whether you seek relaxation, adventure, or a cultural journey, this enchanting island has something for every traveler. Prepare to immerse yourself in the beauty of Anguilla and create memories that will last a lifetime.

History and Cultural background

Anguilla has a rich history that dates back to the indigenous Arawak people who inhabited the island before the arrival of European colonizers. Over the centuries, the island was under the control of various European powers before becoming a British territory in the 19th century. The cultural heritage of Anguilla is a blend of African, European, and indigenous influences, which is reflected in its music, cuisine, and traditions.

Practical information for travelers

Before embarking on your journey to Anguilla, it is important to be aware of practical information that will enhance your travel experience. This includes understanding visa requirements, local currency, and other essential details. Visitors to Anguilla typically do not require a visa for stays of up to 90 days, but it is always advisable to check with your relevant embassy or consulate. The local currency is the Eastern Caribbean dollar (XCD), although US dollars are widely accepted. English is the official language, and the island operates on Atlantic Standard Time (AST).

In the following sections of this travel guide, you will find comprehensive information on how to get to Anguilla, explore its different regions, discover its top attractions, indulge in its culinary delights, engage in outdoor activities, and much more. Whether you are planning a family vacation, a romantic getaway, or an adventure-filled trip, Anguilla has something to offer every type of traveler. So sit back, relax, and let this guide be your companion as you embark on an unforgettable journey to Anguilla Island.

History: Anguilla, a small and stunning island located in the Caribbean Sea, boasts a rich and fascinating history that has shaped its culture and identity. From its early indigenous inhabitants to European colonization and struggles for independence, the story of Anguilla is one of resilience, determination, and cultural diversity. This travel guide aims to provide an elaborate and detailed description of Anguilla's captivating history, allowing visitors to better understand and appreciate the island's heritage.

The earliest known inhabitants of Anguilla were the Amerindians, specifically the Arawak and Carib tribes. These indigenous peoples thrived on the island for centuries, living off the bountiful marine resources and cultivating crops such as corn, yams, and cotton. Evidence of their presence can still be found today in the form of ancient artifacts and petroglyphs.

In 1493, Christopher Columbus arrived in the Caribbean, marking the beginning of European exploration and colonization. Anguilla, along with many other Caribbean islands, fell under Spanish control. However, due to its lack of valuable resources and its remote location, the island remained relatively untouched by Spanish settlement.

In the early 17th century, Anguilla became a haven for pirates who used its secluded coves and hidden bays as bases for their operations. These notorious figures, including the likes of Captain Kidd and Blackbeard, sought refuge on the island while plundering merchant ships in the region. The legacy of piracy is still celebrated today through events like the annual Anguilla Day boat race, where locals commemorate their pirate ancestors.

By the mid-17th century, European powers began to show interest in Anguilla due to its strategic location in the Caribbean. The island changed hands multiple times between the British, French, and Dutch before finally becoming a British colony in 1650. It was during this period that plantation agriculture was introduced, primarily focusing on cotton and indigo production. African slaves were brought to Anguilla to work on these plantations, significantly shaping the island's demographic makeup and culture.

The 19th century saw the decline of the plantation economy in Anguilla, as the abolitionist movement gained momentum and slavery was eventually abolished in the British Empire in 1834. Many former slaves became independent farmers, cultivating crops such as corn, peas, and sweet potatoes. The island's economy also diversified with the introduction of salt production, which became a major industry until the early 20th century.

Anguilla's struggle for self-determination and independence began in the 20th century. In 1967, the island gained separate administrative status from its neighboring island of St. Kitts and Nevis, forming the short-lived "Associated State of St. Kitts-Nevis-Anguilla." However, tensions arose between Anguilla and the central government, leading to a revolution in 1969. British troops were eventually sent to restore order, and Anguilla was placed under direct British rule until 1980 when it became a separate British Overseas Territory.

Since gaining its autonomy, Anguilla has focused on developing its tourism industry, capitalizing on its pristine beaches, crystal-clear waters, and warm hospitality. Today, visitors can explore the island's rich history through its numerous historical sites and landmarks, such as the Wallblake House, a plantation-era mansion turned museum, and the Heritage Collection Museum, which showcases artifacts from Anguilla's past.

Anguilla's history is a tapestry woven with indigenous cultures, European colonization, piracy, slavery, and struggles for independence. This small Caribbean island stands as a testament to the resilience and determination of its people. Understanding and appreciating this rich history enhances the experience of visiting Anguilla, allowing travelers to connect with its vibrant culture and immerse themselves in its captivating past.

Culture: The culture of Anguilla is a vibrant and diverse blend of influences from its indigenous peoples, European settlers, African slaves, and modern-day residents. Visitors to the island can immerse themselves in the local culture through various activities, events, and experiences.

One of the most notable aspects of Anguillian culture is its music and dance. The island has a rich musical heritage, with genres such as calypso, reggae, soca, and traditional folk music being popular among the locals. Visitors can enjoy live performances at local bars, restaurants, and beachside venues, where they can witness the infectious rhythms and energetic dance moves that are an integral part of Anguillian culture.

Art and craft are also significant components of the island's culture. Anguilla is home to numerous talented artists and artisans who create beautiful paintings, sculptures, ceramics, and jewelry inspired by the island's natural beauty and cultural heritage. Visitors can explore art galleries and studios to admire and purchase these unique creations, providing them with a tangible piece of Anguilla's artistic culture.

Culinary experiences are another way to delve into Anguillian culture. The island boasts a diverse culinary scene influenced by African, European, and Caribbean cuisines. Local dishes such as saltfish and Johnny cakes, seafood delicacies like grilled lobster and conch fritters, and refreshing tropical fruits like mangoes and papayas are must-try culinary delights. Visitors can indulge in these flavors at local restaurants, beachside shacks, and food festivals, where they can savor the island's gastronomic offerings while immersing themselves in its culinary traditions.

Religion plays a significant role in Anguillian culture, with Christianity being the dominant faith. The island is home to numerous churches of various denominations, and visitors are welcome to attend services and experience the spiritual side of Anguillian life. Religious festivals and events are also celebrated throughout the year, providing visitors with an opportunity to witness the island's faith-based traditions and customs.

Sports, particularly cricket and boat racing, are deeply ingrained in Anguillian culture. Cricket matches are a common sight on the island, with locals and visitors alike gathering to watch and participate in this beloved sport. Boat racing, a tradition rooted in the island's pirate history, is a thrilling and exhilarating experience. Visitors can witness these races during the annual Anguilla Day boat race, where locals showcase their sailing skills and pay homage to their seafaring ancestors.

The warm and welcoming nature of the Anguillian people is another defining aspect of the island's culture. Visitors will be greeted with genuine hospitality and a friendly smile wherever they go, making them feel at home and fostering a sense of community. Engaging with the locals, participating in community events, and supporting local businesses are excellent ways to connect with Anguillian culture and create lasting memories.

Anguilla's culture is a vibrant tapestry woven with music, art, cuisine, religion, sports, and warm hospitality. Visitors to the island can immerse themselves in this rich cultural heritage through various activities and experiences, allowing them to forge a deeper connection with the island and its people. Exploring and appreciating Anguilla's culture enhances the travel experience, providing a unique and unforgettable journey into the heart and soul of this captivating Caribbean paradise.

Geography and Climate

Geography: Anguilla is a small island located in the eastern Caribbean, just north of St. Martin. It is part of the Leeward Islands in the Lesser Antilles region. The island is known for its stunning beaches, crystal-clear turquoise waters, and tranquil atmosphere.

Geographically, Anguilla is a flat and low-lying island, with its highest point reaching only 213 feet above sea level. The island is approximately 16 miles long and 3 miles wide, covering an area of about 35 square miles. Despite its small size, Anguilla boasts 33 pristine white sand beaches, each with its own unique charm and character.

The coastline of Anguilla is dotted with picturesque coves, bays, and coral reefs, making it a haven for snorkeling, scuba diving, and other water activities. Shoal Bay East, Rendezvous Bay, and Meads Bay are among the most popular beaches on the island, offering pristine sands, calm waters, and breathtaking views.

The island's interior is characterized by rolling hills and fertile valleys, covered in lush vegetation. Palm trees, sea grapes, and flowering plants are abundant, creating a tropical paradise that is perfect for nature lovers. The island's landscape also includes salt ponds, which are an important part of Anguilla's history and culture.

The average temperature ranges from 77°F to 85°F (25°C to 29°C), providing ideal conditions for beach activities and outdoor exploration. The island experiences a dry season from December to April and a wet season from May to November, with rainfall being more frequent during the latter period.

The island's geography also includes several small offshore islands and cays, such as Scrub Island, Dog Island, and Prickly Pear Cays. These uninhabited islands are popular destinations for day trips and offer secluded beaches and excellent snorkeling opportunities.

Getting to Anguilla is relatively easy, with regular flights from major international airports in the Caribbean, the United States, and Europe. The island is also accessible by ferry from neighboring islands, such as St. Martin.

Once on the island, transportation options include rental cars, taxis, and bicycles. The main road on Anguilla, known as the Queen Elizabeth II Highway, runs from one end of the island to the other, making it easy to explore the various beaches and attractions.

Anguilla's geography is characterized by its stunning beaches, tranquil waters, and lush vegetation. The island's small size and flat terrain make it easily accessible and perfect for exploring. Whether you're looking to relax on pristine sands, snorkel in crystal-clear waters, or immerse yourself in nature, Anguilla offers a captivating and unforgettable experience for travelers and tourists.

Climate: Anguilla has a tropical climate, characterized by warm temperatures and consistent trade winds. The island experiences two main seasons: a dry season from December to April and a wet season from May to November.

During the dry season, Anguilla enjoys plenty of sunshine and minimal rainfall. The average temperature ranges from 77°F to 85°F (25°C to 29°C), providing ideal conditions for beach activities and outdoor exploration. The humidity is relatively low during this time, making it comfortable for visitors.

The wet season in Anguilla, from May to November, sees an increase in rainfall and higher humidity levels. However, it is important to note that even during the wet season, the rain showers are usually brief and do not last all day. Rainfall is more frequent in the form of short, intense showers or thunderstorms, followed by clear skies.

The average annual rainfall in Anguilla is around 35 inches (890 mm), with the highest levels occurring in September and October. These months are considered the peak of the hurricane season in the

Caribbean, although Anguilla is generally not as prone to direct hits from hurricanes as other islands in the region. It is still advisable to monitor weather updates and be prepared for any potential storms during this time.

The trade winds that blow across Anguilla help to keep the temperatures comfortable throughout the year. These winds provide a refreshing breeze, making it pleasant to be outdoors even on warmer days. The water temperature also remains warm, ranging from 78°F to 84°F (26°C to 29°C), perfect for swimming, snorkeling, and other water activities.

Overall, Anguilla's climate is favorable for year-round travel. Whether you visit during the dry season for guaranteed sunshine or during the wet season to experience the island's lush greenery, you can expect warm temperatures and a tropical atmosphere. It is always a good idea to pack sunscreen, lightweight clothing, and rain gear to be prepared for any weather conditions during your stay in Anguilla

Travel Tips and Advice

When planning a trip to Anguilla, it is important to consider the island's tropical climate and pack accordingly. Here are some travel tips and advice to help you make the most of your visit:

Pack lightweight and breathable clothing: Due to the warm temperatures year-round, it is best to pack lightweight and breathable clothing such as cotton or linen. This will enable you have a pleasant stay during heat and humidity

Don't forget your sunscreen: With plenty of sunshine throughout the year, it is crucial to protect your skin from the sun's harmful rays. Pack a high SPF sunscreen and apply it regularly, especially if you plan on spending time at the beach or engaging in outdoor activities.

Stay hydrated: The warm temperatures and humidity can cause dehydration, so it is important to drink plenty of water. Endeavor to stay hydrated by always having water around you.

Be prepared for rain showers: While the wet season in Anguilla brings increased rainfall, the showers are usually brief and do not last all day. However, it is still advisable to pack a lightweight rain jacket or umbrella to be prepared for any sudden downpours.

Monitor weather updates: During the peak of the hurricane season in September and October, it is important to stay informed about any potential storms or hurricanes. Monitor weather updates regularly and follow any instructions or advisories given by local authorities.

Embrace the trade winds: The consistent trade winds in Anguilla provide a refreshing breeze, making it pleasant to be outdoors even on warmer days. Take advantage of this natural air conditioning and enjoy the island's outdoor activities.

Explore the island's natural beauty: Whether you visit during the dry season or wet season, Anguilla offers stunning natural beauty. From pristine beaches to lush greenery, there is plenty to explore and discover. Take advantage of the ideal conditions for beach activities, snorkeling, and outdoor exploration.

Respect the local culture: Anguilla is known for its friendly and welcoming locals. Take the time to learn about the island's culture and customs, and always show respect to the people and their traditions.

Support local businesses: Anguilla relies heavily on tourism, so consider supporting local businesses during your visit. Whether it's dining at local restaurants or purchasing souvenirs from local artisans, your support can make a positive impact on the community.

Relax and enjoy the island life: Anguilla is known for its laid-back and relaxing atmosphere. Take the time to unwind, soak up the sun, and embrace the island's tropical vibes. Whether you choose to lounge on the beach or indulge in a spa treatment, make sure to take some time for yourself and enjoy the beauty of Anguilla.

By following these travel tips and advice, you can have a memorable and enjoyable trip to Anguilla.

Chapter One: Getting to Anguilla

Transportation options

To get to Anguilla Island, there are several options available. The most common way is to fly into Clayton J. Lloyd International Airport (AXA), which is the island's only airport. From that point, you can take a taxi or lease a vehicle to arrive at your convenience.

If you are flying from the United States, there are direct flights available from major cities such as Miami, New York, and Atlanta. These flights are operated by airlines like American Airlines, Delta Air Lines, and JetBlue Airways. The period of the flight is normally 3-4 hours.

If you are coming from other international destinations, you can fly to neighboring islands such as Puerto Rico or St. Maarten and then take a connecting flight or ferry to Anguilla. There are regular ferry services from St. Maarten to Anguilla, with a journey time of approximately 25 minutes.

Another option for getting to Anguilla is by private boat or yacht. The island has several marinas and harbors where you can dock your boat. Customs and immigration procedures will need to be followed upon arrival.

Once you have arrived in Anguilla, transportation on the island is relatively easy. Taxis are promptly accessible at the air terminal and all through the island.

Rental cars are also popular, and there are several car rental agencies to choose from. Driving is on the left-hand side of the road, as Anguilla is a British territory.

It is important to note that there are no direct flights from Europe or Canada to Anguilla. Travelers from these regions will need to fly to a nearby island and then take a connecting flight or ferry.

Generally, getting to Anguilla Island is relatively straightforward, with options for both air and sea travel. Whether you choose to fly directly or take a more scenic route via neighboring islands, the journey to Anguilla is well worth it for the stunning beaches and warm hospitality that await you.

Information on nearby international airports and their connections

If you are flying from the United States, there are direct flights available from major cities such as Miami, New York, and Atlanta. Airlines like American Airlines, Delta Air Lines, and JetBlue Airways operate these flights, with a typical duration of 3-4 hours.

For travelers coming from other international destinations, flying to neighboring islands such as Puerto Rico or St. Maarten is a common option. From there, you can take a connecting flight or ferry to Anguilla. Regular ferry services are available from St. Maarten to Anguilla, with a journey time of approximately 25 minutes.

Tips for navigating local transportation within Anguilla

Once you have arrived in Anguilla, transportation on the island is relatively easy. Taxis are promptly accessible at the air terminal and all through the island. They are a convenient option for getting around if you don't want to rent a car.

If you prefer to have more flexibility and independence, rental cars are popular on the island.

There are several car rental agencies to choose from, and driving is on the left-hand side of the road, as Anguilla is a British territory. It's important to note that a temporary driving permit is required, which can be obtained at the rental agency or at the police station.

In terms of navigating the island, Anguilla has well-maintained roads and signage, making it easy to get around. The island is relatively small, with a total area of 35 square miles, so it's not difficult to explore different parts of the island.

If you prefer a more leisurely and scenic mode of transportation, you can also consider renting a bicycle or scooter to explore the island at your own pace. This can be a great way to enjoy the beautiful beaches and take in the stunning views.

Overall, getting around Anguilla is relatively straightforward, whether you choose to rely on taxis, rental cars, or alternative modes of transportation. The island is known for its friendly and welcoming locals, so don't hesitate to ask for directions or recommendations if needed.

Chapter Two: Exploring the Regions of Anguilla

The main regions and towns in Anguilla

Anguilla is divided into seven main regions, each offering its own unique charm and attractions. The main regions and towns in Anguilla include:

The Valley: The Valley is the capital of Anguilla and serves as the administrative and commercial hub of the island. It is home to government buildings, banks, shops, and restaurants.

West End: Located on the western tip of the island, West End is known for its stunning sunsets and beautiful beaches. It is also home to luxury resorts and villas, making it a popular destination for tourists.

East End: The eastern part of Anguilla is less developed and offers a more tranquil and secluded experience. It is home to pristine beaches, including Shoal Bay East, which is often ranked as one of the best beaches in the Caribbean.

Sandy Ground: Sandy Ground is a vibrant and lively area known for its beach bars, live music, and nightlife. It is a popular spot for locals and tourists alike, especially during the weekends.

Shoal Bay: Shoal Bay is another popular region in Anguilla, famous for its crystal-clear turquoise waters and powdery white sand beaches. It offers a range of water sports activities and beachfront dining options.

Meads Bay: Meads Bay is known for its upscale resorts and luxury accommodations. It boasts a beautiful stretch of beach with calm waters, perfect for swimming and snorkeling.

Rendezvous Bay: Rendezvous Bay is a secluded and peaceful region with a long stretch of pristine beach. It offers a more laid-back atmosphere and is ideal for relaxation and tranquility.

Highlighting popular attractions and activities in each region

The Valley: While The Valley is primarily a business hub, visitors can explore historical sites such as the Wallblake House, a restored plantation house, and the Heritage Collection Museum, which showcases Anguilla's history and culture.

West End: West End is home to beautiful beaches like Barnes Bay and Meads Bay, where visitors can relax, swim, and enjoy water sports activities. The Dolphin Discovery Anguilla, located in West End, offers the opportunity to swim with dolphins.

East End: The main attraction in the East End region is Shoal Bay East, known for its stunning turquoise waters and powdery white sand. It is a popular spot for snorkeling and swimming.

Sandy Ground: Sandy Ground is famous for its beach bars and live music scene. Visitors can enjoy drinks, local cuisine, and live performances at popular venues like Johnno's Beach Stop and Elvis' Beach Bar.

Shoal Bay: In addition to its beautiful beach, Shoal Bay offers a range of water sports activities such as snorkeling, kayaking, and paddleboarding. Visitors can also enjoy beachfront dining at popular restaurants like Zemi Beach House Resort & Spa.

Meads Bay: Meads Bay is known for its luxury resorts and upscale dining options. Visitors can indulge in spa treatments, fine dining experiences, and enjoy the calm waters of the bay.

Rendezvous Bay: Rendezvous Bay offers a peaceful and secluded beach experience. Visitors can relax on the beach, take long walks along the shoreline, or enjoy a picnic in a tranquil setting.

Recommendations for accommodations, dining, and shopping in different areas

The Valley: While The Valley is primarily a business district, there are a few accommodations available for those who prefer to stay in the capital. Options include guesthouses and small hotels. Dining options range from local eateries to international cuisine, and there are some shops and boutiques for shopping.

West End: West End offers a range of luxury accommodations including resorts, villas, and boutique hotels. Dining options include beachfront restaurants serving fresh seafood and international cuisine. There are also a few shops and boutiques for shopping.

East End: Accommodations in the East End tend to be more secluded and offer a peaceful retreat. There are a few small hotels and villas available. Dining options are limited, but visitors can enjoy local cuisine

Overall, Anguilla offers a range of accommodations, dining options, and shopping experiences in each region, catering to different preferences and budgets.

Chapter Three: Top Attractions in Anguilla

Iconic beaches and beach activities in Anguilla:

Anguilla is renowned for its pristine beaches, boasting crystal-clear turquoise waters and powdery white sand. Some of the iconic beaches in Anguilla include:

Shoal Bay East: Considered one of the best beaches in the Caribbean, Shoal Bay East stretches for two miles and offers breathtaking views. Visitors can relax on the soft sand, swim in the calm waters, and indulge in water sports activities such as snorkeling, kayaking, and paddleboarding.

Meads Bay: Meads Bay is known for its calm waters and luxurious resorts. The beach offers a tranquil setting for sunbathing, swimming, and enjoying water sports activities. Visitors can also find beachfront dining options serving delicious seafood and refreshing cocktails.

Rendezvous Bay: Rendezvous Bay is a secluded and peaceful beach that stretches for two miles. It is an ideal place for those looking for pleasure and a serene environment. Visitors can take long walks along the shoreline, enjoy a picnic on the beach, or simply soak up the sun.

Sandy Ground: While Sandy Ground is primarily known for its lively nightlife scene, it also offers a beautiful beach. Visitors can relax on the sand, swim in the clear waters, and enjoy beach bars and restaurants that line the shore.

Barnes Bay: Barnes Bay is a hidden gem with pristine waters and a quiet atmosphere. It is less crowded compared to other beaches on the island, making it perfect for those seeking privacy. Visitors can enjoy swimming, snorkeling, and sunbathing in a peaceful setting.

Water sports and recreational activities (snorkeling, sailing, etc.)

Anguilla offers a wide range of water sports and recreational activities for adventure enthusiasts. Some popular activities include:

Snorkeling: With its clear waters and vibrant marine life, Anguilla is a paradise for snorkelers. Visitors can explore coral reefs, swim alongside tropical fish, and even encounter sea turtles. Popular snorkeling spots include Little Bay, Shoal Bay East, and Sandy Island.

Sailing: Anguilla's calm and warm waters make it an ideal destination for sailing. Visitors can rent sailboats or catamarans and explore the coastline, discovering hidden coves and secluded beaches. Sunset sailing trips are particularly popular, offering breathtaking views of the Caribbean Sea.

Kayaking: Kayaking is a great way to explore Anguilla's coastline and discover hidden gems. Visitors can rent kayaks and paddle along the shore, exploring secluded beaches and coves. Kayaking tours are also available, allowing visitors to explore mangroves and spot local wildlife.

Jet Skiing: For those seeking a thrilling water adventure, jet skiing is a popular activity in Anguilla. Visitors can rent jet skis and zoom across the turquoise waters, enjoying the adrenaline rush and breathtaking views of the coastline.

Stand-up   Paddleboarding: Stand-up paddleboarding (SUP) is a popular activity in Anguilla, offering a unique way to explore the island's waters. Visitors can rent SUP boards and paddle along the calm bays, enjoying the tranquility and beautiful scenery.

Cultural and historical landmarks to visit (museums, art galleries, etc.)

Anguilla has a rich cultural and historical heritage, with several landmarks worth visiting. Some notable cultural and historical attractions include:

Heritage Collection Museum: Located in The Valley, the Heritage Collection Museum showcases Anguilla's history and culture through exhibits of artifacts, photographs, and artwork. Visitors can learn about the island's indigenous people, colonial history, and cultural traditions.

Wallblake House: The Wallblake House is a restored plantation house dating back to the 18th century. It is one of the few surviving plantation houses in the Caribbean and offers a glimpse into Anguilla's colonial past. Visitors can explore the house's architecture, gardens, and learn about the island's sugar cane industry.

Cheddie Richardson Carving Studio: Cheddie Richardson is a renowned local artist known for his wood carvings. His studio in The Valley showcases his intricate carvings, depicting scenes from Anguillian life and culture. Visitors can witness the artist at work and purchase unique pieces of art.

Devonish Art Gallery: The Devonish Art Gallery in West End showcases the works of local artist Courtney Devonish. His vibrant and colorful paintings depict scenes of Anguillian life, culture, and nature. Visitors can admire and purchase these unique pieces of art.

Nature reserves and hiking trails for outdoor enthusiasts

Anguilla offers nature reserves and hiking trails for outdoor enthusiasts to explore its natural beauty. Some notable reserves and trails include:

East End Pond: East End Pond is a designated Ramsar site and a haven for birdwatchers. It is home to a diverse range of bird species, including herons, egrets, and flamingos. Visitors can explore the reserve on foot or by kayak, observing the rich birdlife in their natural habitat.

Katouche Bay: Katouche Bay is a protected area that offers a scenic hiking trail through lush vegetation and coastal cliffs. The trail leads to a secluded beach, offering a rewarding experience for hikers. Visitors can also spot native plants and wildlife along the way.

Cove Bay Trail: The Cove Bay Trail is a coastal trail that offers stunning views of the coastline and the Caribbean Sea. It is an easy hike suitable for all fitness levels, allowing visitors to enjoy the natural beauty of Anguilla.

Local festivals and events worth experiencing for a travel guide to Anguilla as a tourist

Anguilla is known for its vibrant festivals and events that showcase the island's culture, music, and cuisine. Some popular festivals and events include:

Anguilla Summer Festival: The Anguilla Summer Festival is a week-long celebration held in August. It features live music performances, parades, beauty pageants, and various cultural events. Visitors can immerse themselves in the lively atmosphere and experience the island's vibrant culture.

Moonsplash Music Festival: The Moonsplash Music Festival is an annual event held in March on the beautiful beaches of Anguilla. It features live music performances by local and international artists, showcasing a variety of genres including reggae, soca, and jazz. Visitors can enjoy the music, dance, and celebrate under the moonlit sky.

Tranquility Jazz Festival: The Tranquility Jazz Festival is a three-day event held in November, showcasing the best of jazz music. Visitors can enjoy live performances by local and international jazz artists in various venues across the island.

Lit Fest: The Anguilla Lit Fest is a literary festival held in May, attracting renowned authors, poets, and literary enthusiasts from around the world. It features panel discussions, book signings, workshops, and poetry readings. Visitors can engage with authors, discover new literature, and celebrate the written word.

Boat Racing: Boat racing is a popular sport in Anguilla, and several regattas are held throughout the year. These events showcase the island's seafaring heritage and offer thrilling races between locally built wooden sailboats. Visitors can witness the excitement and cheer for their favorite teams during these regattas.

Attending these festivals and events allows tourists to immerse themselves in Anguilla's vibrant culture, music, and traditions.

Chapter Four: Dining and Nightlife in Anguilla

Anguilla's culinary scene and local specialties

Anguilla is renowned for its vibrant culinary scene, offering a diverse range of dining options that cater to all tastes and preferences. The island's cuisine is influenced by its Caribbean roots, with a focus on fresh seafood, flavorful spices, and local ingredients. Visitors to Anguilla can expect a delightful culinary journey, exploring both fine dining establishments and local eateries.

One of the local specialties that visitors must try is the Anguillian lobster. The island is known for its succulent and flavorful lobsters, which are typically grilled or served in rich butter sauce. Another local delicacy is conch, a type of sea snail that is often used in soups, salads, and fritters. Visitors can also indulge in dishes such as jerk chicken, curried goat, and fresh fish prepared in various styles.

In addition to traditional Caribbean fare, Anguilla's culinary scene also offers international cuisines, including French, Italian, Asian, and Mediterranean. Many restaurants on the island pride themselves on using locally sourced ingredients and showcasing the flavors of Anguilla.

Recommendations for fine dining restaurants and local eateries

Anguilla boasts a number of fine dining establishments that offer exquisite cuisine and breathtaking views. Here are some recommendations for fine dining restaurants in Anguilla:

Blanchards: Located on Meads Bay, Blanchards is a renowned restaurant that has been serving delicious cuisine for over 20 years. The menu features a fusion of Caribbean and international flavors, with dishes such as grilled local lobster, seared scallops, and herb-crusted rack of lamb. The restaurant offers a romantic beachfront setting and impeccable service.

Veya: Situated in Sandy Ground, Veya is known for its innovative Caribbean cuisine with global influences. The menu features dishes such as coconut-crusted grouper, jerk-spiced duck breast, and plantain-crusted snapper. The restaurant offers a vibrant and colorful atmosphere, with live music performances adding to the overall experience.

Straw Hat: Located on Meads Bay, Straw Hat offers a blend of Caribbean and international flavors in a relaxed beachfront setting. The menu features dishes such as grilled shrimp with mango salsa, coconut-crusted mahi-mahi, and jerk chicken. Visitors can enjoy their meal while taking in the stunning views of the turquoise waters.

For those looking to experience local eateries and street food, here are some recommendations:

Ken's BBQ: Located in The Valley, Ken's BBQ is a popular spot for locals and tourists alike. They serve delicious barbecued meats such as ribs, chicken, and pork, along with traditional sides like rice and peas, plantains, and coleslaw. Visitors can enjoy their meal in a casual and friendly atmosphere.

Geraud's Patisserie: Situated in Sandy Ground, Geraud's Patisserie is a French bakery that offers a range of delectable pastries, croissants, and bread. Visitors can indulge in freshly baked goods and enjoy a cup of coffee or tea in a cozy setting.

Smokey's at the Cove: Located in Cove Bay, Smokey's at the Cove is a laid-back beach bar and restaurant that serves Caribbean-inspired dishes. Visitors can enjoy dishes such as grilled fish sandwiches, conch fritters, and jerk chicken while taking in the beautiful views of the beach.

Information on beach bars, lounges, and nightlife hotspots

Anguilla offers a vibrant nightlife scene with a variety of beach bars, lounges, and nightlife hotspots. Here are some recommendations for experiencing the nightlife in Anguilla:

Elvis' Beach Bar: Located on Sandy Ground Beach, Elvis' Beach Bar is a popular spot for live music and dancing. Visitors can enjoy a refreshing cocktail, listen to local bands playing reggae and soca music, and dance the night away on the sandy dance floor.

The Dune Preserve: Situated on Rendezvous Bay, The Dune Preserve is a beach bar and live music venue owned by reggae artist Bankie Banx. Visitors can enjoy live performances by local and international musicians, sip on rum punch, and soak up the laid-back atmosphere.

The Pumphouse: Located in Sandy Ground, The Pumphouse is a historic building that has been converted into a lively bar and restaurant. It offers live music, karaoke nights, and a wide selection of drinks. Visitors can enjoy the vibrant atmosphere and mingle with locals and tourists alike.

SandBar: Situated on Sandy Ground Beach, SandBar is a beachfront lounge that offers stunning sunset views and a relaxed ambiance. Visitors can enjoy a variety of cocktails, listen to live music, and unwind in a comfortable setting.

Bankie Banx's Dune Preserve - Rendezvous Bay: Bankie Banx's Dune Preserve is a legendary beach bar located on Rendezvous Bay. It offers live music performances, delicious drinks, and a unique atmosphere created by the eclectic decorations made from driftwood and other found objects.

These beach bars, lounges, and nightlife hotspots offer visitors the opportunity to experience Anguilla's vibrant nightlife scene while enjoying the island's beautiful beaches and stunning views.

Chapter Five: Outdoor Activities in Anguilla

Watersports opportunities (kayaking, paddleboarding, etc.)

Anguilla offers a wide range of watersports activities for visitors to enjoy its crystal-clear turquoise waters. One popular activity is kayaking, where tourists can explore the island's coastline and secluded beaches at their own pace. Kayak rentals are available at various locations, and guided tours are also offered for those who prefer a more structured experience.

Paddleboarding is another popular watersport in Anguilla, allowing visitors to glide across the calm waters while enjoying the stunning views. Whether you're a beginner or an experienced paddler, there are rental shops and tour operators that offer paddleboarding lessons and guided tours.

For those seeking a more adventurous experience, Anguilla also offers activities such as jet skiing, parasailing, and windsurfing. Jet skiing allows visitors to speed across the waves and explore the island's coastline, while parasailing offers a unique perspective of Anguilla from high above the water. Windsurfing enthusiasts can take advantage of the island's steady trade winds and enjoy an exhilarating ride on the waves.

Snorkeling and diving are also popular activities in Anguilla, thanks to its vibrant coral reefs and diverse marine life. Visitors can rent snorkeling gear and explore the underwater world on their own or join a guided snorkeling tour to discover the best spots. Diving enthusiasts can explore Anguilla's numerous dive sites, which range from shallow reefs to deeper wrecks and walls. There are several dive operators on the island that offer certification courses, guided dives, and equipment rentals.

Sailing and boat excursions around the island

Anguilla's stunning coastline and surrounding islands make it a perfect destination for sailing and boat excursions. Visitors can rent sailboats, catamarans, or yachts to explore the island's hidden coves, pristine beaches, and secluded islands.

One popular sailing excursion is a trip to Prickly Pear Cays, a small group of uninhabited islands located off the northwest coast of Anguilla. Visitors can anchor in the calm waters and enjoy snorkeling, swimming, and sunbathing on the pristine beaches. Some boat excursions also include a beach barbecue, where visitors can indulge in delicious grilled seafood and local specialties.

Another popular destination for boat excursions is Sandy Island, a tiny island located off Sandy Ground Beach. Visitors can take a short boat ride to the island and spend the day relaxing on the white sandy beaches, snorkeling in the clear waters, and enjoying a meal at the beachfront restaurant.

For those looking to explore further afield, boat excursions to neighboring islands such as St. Martin/St. Maarten, St. Barthélemy, and Saba are also available. These excursions allow visitors to experience the unique culture, cuisine, and landscapes of these nearby islands.

Golf courses and tennis facilities

Although Anguilla is a small island, it offers excellent golf and tennis facilities for sports enthusiasts. The CuisinArt Golf Resort and Spa flaunts a 18-opening title fairway planned by Greg Norman.This par-72 course offers stunning ocean views and challenging holes that cater to both beginners and experienced golfers. The resort also provides golf lessons, equipment rentals, and a pro shop.

For tennis enthusiasts, the Anguilla Tennis Academy is a popular destination. Located in Blowing Point, this state-of-the-art facility offers six hard courts and two clay courts. Visitors can book court time, take private lessons, or join group clinics. The academy also hosts tournaments and events throughout the year.

Additionally, many resorts and hotels on the island have their own tennis courts available for guests to use. These facilities provide a great opportunity for visitors to stay active and enjoy a friendly game of tennis while soaking up the island's beautiful surroundings.

Yoga retreats and wellness centers

Anguilla is also known for its wellness offerings, with several yoga retreats and wellness centers available for visitors seeking relaxation and rejuvenation. These retreats and centers offer a serene environment, expert instructors, and a range of wellness activities.

One popular yoga retreat is The Yoga Retreat at The Reef by CuisinArt. Located on Merrywing Bay, this retreat offers daily yoga classes, meditation sessions, and wellness workshops. Visitors can choose from a variety of yoga styles, including Vinyasa, Hatha, and Yin, and enjoy the tranquil surroundings of the resort.

The Zemi Beach House Resort & Spa is another wellness destination in Anguilla. The resort's spa offers a range of holistic treatments, including massages, facials, and body scrubs. They also have a dedicated yoga deck where guests can participate in daily yoga classes overlooking the Caribbean Sea.

In addition to these retreats, many resorts and hotels on the island offer wellness facilities such as fitness centers, spas, and wellness programs. Visitors can indulge in massages, facials, and other spa treatments, or participate in fitness classes and personal training sessions to maintain their well-being during their stay in Anguilla.

Chapter Six: Shopping and Souvenirs in Anguilla

Overview of local markets, boutiques, and shopping centers

Anguilla may be a small island, but it offers a variety of shopping options for visitors looking to take home unique souvenirs and local crafts. While the island does not have large shopping centers or malls, there are several local markets and boutiques where tourists can find a range of goods.

The most popular market on the island is the Anguilla Arts and Crafts Center, located in The Valley. This vibrant market showcases the work of local artisans and craftsmen, offering a wide selection of handmade goods such as pottery, paintings, jewelry, wood carvings, and woven baskets. Visitors can browse through the stalls and interact with the artists themselves, gaining insight into the creative process and the island's culture.

Another must-visit market is the Saturday Morning Market in The Valley. Held every Saturday from 8 am to 12 pm, this bustling market is a hub of activity where locals and tourists come together. Here, visitors can find fresh produce, local spices, homemade jams and sauces, handmade soaps, and other locally produced goods. It's a great place to immerse yourself in the local community and experience the vibrant atmosphere of Anguilla.

In addition to these markets, there are also several boutiques scattered across the island that offer a range of clothing, accessories, and home decor. Some popular boutiques include Limin', Sea Spray Boutique, and Irie Life. These boutiques showcase local designers as well as international brands, providing visitors with a unique shopping experience.

Recommendations for unique souvenirs and local crafts

When it comes to unique souvenirs and local crafts, Anguilla offers a variety of options that capture the essence of the island. Here are some recommendations for souvenirs that are worth considering:

Handmade pottery: Anguilla is known for its pottery, and visitors can find beautifully crafted ceramic pieces that reflect the island's vibrant colors and natural beauty. Look for bowls, vases, and decorative items adorned with intricate designs and patterns.

Shell jewelry: Anguilla is home to stunning beaches, and its shores are often littered with beautiful seashells. Local artisans transform these shells into unique pieces of jewelry, including necklaces, bracelets, and earrings. These pieces serve as a reminder of the island's natural beauty.

Local spices and sauces: Anguilla is known for its flavorful cuisine, and visitors can bring a taste of the island home by purchasing local spices and sauces. Look for blends of Caribbean spices, hot sauces made from local peppers, and fruit preserves made from tropical fruits.

Woven baskets: Anguilla has a rich tradition of basket weaving, and visitors can find intricately woven baskets made from natural materials such as palm leaves and straw. These baskets make for practical and decorative souvenirs.

Paintings and artwork: Anguilla is home to a thriving arts scene, and visitors can find a wide range of paintings and artwork that capture the island's beauty. Look for pieces that depict the turquoise waters, sandy beaches, and vibrant landscapes of Anguilla.

Tips for bargaining and shopping etiquette in Anguilla

While bargaining is not common practice in Anguilla, there are a few tips to keep in mind when shopping on the island:

Respect local customs: When visiting markets or boutiques, it's important to respect local customs and traditions. Greet shopkeepers with a friendly "good morning" or "good afternoon," and engage in polite conversation before discussing prices.

Compare prices: Before making a purchase, it's a good idea to compare prices at different stalls or shops to ensure you're getting a fair deal. This allows you to gauge the average price for an item and make an informed decision.

Ask about the story behind the item: Many local crafts and souvenirs in Anguilla have a story or cultural significance behind them. Take the time to ask the shopkeeper about the item's origin or how it was made. This not only enhances your shopping experience but also supports local artisans.

Be polite and patient: Shopping in Anguilla is a relaxed affair, so it's important to be patient and polite when interacting with shopkeepers. Avoid rushing or pressuring them, and be open to browsing and exploring the different items available.

Support local businesses: Whenever possible, try to support local businesses and artisans by purchasing their products. This not only helps the local economy but also ensures that you're taking home authentic and unique souvenirs from Anguilla.

By following these tips, you can have an enjoyable and respectful shopping experience in Anguilla while supporting the local community.

Chapter Seven: Practical Information for Visitors

Essential travel tips and safety precautions

When visiting Anguilla, it's important to keep the following travel tips and safety precautions in mind:

Travel documents: Ensure that you have a valid passport with at least six months' validity remaining before your planned departure date. Some nationalities may also require a visa to enter Anguilla, so check the visa requirements before traveling.

Safety precautions: Anguilla is generally a safe destination for tourists, but it's always important to take basic safety precautions. Avoid walking alone in isolated areas at night and keep an eye on your belongings in public places. It's also advisable to use reputable transportation services and be cautious when accepting rides from strangers.

Medical insurance: It is highly recommended to have travel medical insurance that covers any medical emergencies or treatment during your stay in Anguilla. This will provide peace of mind and ensure that you are adequately covered in case of any unforeseen circumstances.

Sun protection: Anguilla has a tropical climate, so it's important to protect yourself from the sun. Wear sunscreen with a high SPF, a hat, sunglasses, and lightweight clothing to prevent sunburn and heatstroke.

Water safety: While tap water in Anguilla is generally safe to drink, it's advisable to stick to bottled water to avoid any potential stomach upsets. When swimming, be aware of strong currents and follow any safety guidelines provided by lifeguards or beach authorities.

Emergency contact information: Familiarize yourself with the local emergency contact numbers, including those for the police, ambulance services, and your country's embassy or consulate in Anguilla. Keep these numbers handy in case of any emergencies.

Health and medical services available in Anguilla

Anguilla has a well-developed healthcare system that provides quality medical services to residents and visitors. The main medical facility on the island is the Princess Alexandra Hospital, located in The Valley. This hospital offers a range of services, including emergency care, general medical treatment, and specialist consultations.

In addition to the hospital, there are several private medical clinics and pharmacies scattered across the island. These clinics provide general medical services, vaccinations, and medication prescriptions. It's advisable to carry any necessary prescription medications with you, as not all medications may be readily available on the island.

It's also recommended to have travel medical insurance that covers any medical emergencies or treatment during your stay in Anguilla. This will ensure that you receive the necessary care without incurring substantial out-of-pocket expenses.

Currency exchange and banking facilities

The official currency of Anguilla is the Eastern Caribbean dollar (XCD). However, US dollars are widely accepted throughout the island, and many businesses also accept major credit cards.

There are several banks and ATMs located in The Valley and other major towns on the island where visitors can exchange currency or withdraw cash. It's advisable to inform your bank of your travel plans to Anguilla to avoid any issues with your cards while abroad.

Communication options (internet, mobile networks, etc.)

Anguilla has a reliable telecommunications network, offering a range of communication options for visitors. Most hotels and resorts provide free Wi-Fi for guests, and there are also internet cafes available in major towns.

Mobile networks in Anguilla operate on GSM technology, so visitors with unlocked GSM phones can purchase a local SIM card to use during their stay. Digicel and Flow are the main mobile network providers on the island, offering prepaid SIM cards and data plans for tourists.

Weather patterns and best times to visit Anguilla

In the entire year, Anguilla is known for her tropical climate with warm temperatures. The island experiences a dry season from December to April and a wet season from May to November.

The best opportunity to visit Anguilla is during the dry season, when the weather conditions are radiant and precipitation is negligible. This is likewise the pinnacle vacationer season, so anticipate more exorbitant costs and bigger groups. The months of December to April offer ideal beach weather, with temperatures ranging from the mid-70s to mid-80s Fahrenheit (mid-20s to low 30s Celsius).

The wet season in Anguilla brings higher humidity and occasional showers or thunderstorms. While it may rain during this time, it typically doesn't last long and doesn't significantly impact travel plans. The wet season also offers lower hotel rates and fewer tourists, making it a good option for budget travelers.

Overall, Anguilla can be visited year-round, but the dry season is generally considered the best time to enjoy the island's beaches and outdoor activities.

Chapter Eight: Local Customs and Etiquette

Anguillian culture and customs

Anguilla is a small island in the Caribbean with a rich cultural heritage influenced by African, European, and indigenous traditions. The local culture is vibrant and welcoming, and visitors are encouraged to embrace and respect the customs of the island.

Music and dance play a significant role in Anguillian culture. The island is known for its lively calypso, reggae, and soca music, which can be heard at various festivals and events throughout the year. Traditional dances, such as the Quadrille and the Dinki Mini, are also performed during cultural celebrations.

The Anguillian cooking is a combination of African, European, and Caribbean flavors. Local dishes often include seafood, such as lobster, conch, and fish, as well as rice, peas, and plantains. Visitors should try traditional dishes like "saltfish and johnny cakes" or "anguillan crayfish stew" to experience the local flavors.

Anguilla is also home to a number of historical sites and museums that offer insights into the island's past. The Heritage Collection Museum showcases artifacts and exhibits related to Anguilla's history, while the Wallblake House provides a glimpse into the island's colonial past.

Etiquette tips for interacting with locals

When visiting Anguilla, it's important to respect the local customs and etiquette. Here are a few ways to collaborate with local people

Greetings: Anguillians are generally friendly and warm. It's customary to greet people with a smile and a friendly "good morning" or "good afternoon." Handshakes are also common when meeting someone for the first time.

Politeness: Politeness is highly valued in Anguillian culture. It's important to use "please" and "thank you" when interacting with locals. Being respectful and patient will go a long way in building positive relationships.

Dress code: While Anguilla has a relaxed atmosphere, it's important to dress modestly when visiting public places, such as churches or government buildings. Beachwear is acceptable on the beach, but it's advisable to cover up when leaving the beach area.

Punctuality: Anguillians value punctuality, so it's important to be on time for meetings or appointments. However, it's also worth noting that the island operates on "island time," which means that things may not always run on schedule. It is important to be easygoing and not rigid.

Respect for elders: Respect for elders is an important aspect of Anguillian culture. It's customary to address older individuals with titles such as "Mr." or "Mrs." and to show deference and respect towards them.

Cultural do's and don'ts in Anguilla:

To ensure a respectful and enjoyable experience in Anguilla, here are some cultural do's and don'ts to keep in mind:

Do's:
- Do greet people with a smile and a friendly greeting.
- Do try local cuisine and traditional dishes.
- Do respect local customs and traditions.

- Do ask for permission before taking photos of people or their property.
- Do engage in conversations with locals and show interest in their culture.

Don'ts:
- Don't litter or disrespect the environment. Anguilla is known for its pristine beaches and natural beauty, so it's important to keep the island clean.
- Don't touch or handle someone's personal belongings without permission.
- Don't use offensive language or gestures.
- Don't wear revealing or inappropriate clothing in public places.
- Don't criticize or make negative comments about the local culture or customs.

By following these etiquette tips and respecting the local customs, visitors can have a positive and enriching experience in Anguilla while fostering cultural understanding and appreciation.

Chapter Nine: Traveling with Family or as a Couple

Family-friendly activities and attractions in Anguilla

Anguilla offers a range of family-friendly activities and attractions that cater to travelers of all ages. Here are some popular options:

Beaches: Anguilla is renowned for its pristine beaches with crystal-clear waters and soft white sand. Families can spend quality time together building sandcastles, swimming, snorkeling, or simply relaxing under the sun. Some family-friendly beaches include Shoal Bay East, Meads Bay, and Rendezvous Bay.

Water sports: Anguilla offers various water sports activities that are suitable for families. Families can enjoy kayaking, paddleboarding, jet skiing, or even take a boat tour to explore the island's coastline and nearby cays. Many resorts and water sports companies provide equipment rental and guided tours.

Dolphin Discovery: Located at Blowing Point, Dolphin Discovery offers an interactive experience for families. Visitors can swim with dolphins, learn about their behavior, and even participate in training sessions. This is a unique opportunity for children and adults alike to get up close and personal with these magnificent creatures.

Heritage Collection Museum: For families interested in history and culture, a visit to the Heritage Collection Museum is a must. The museum showcases artifacts and exhibits related to Anguilla's history, including the island's indigenous people, African heritage, and colonial past. It provides an educational experience for children while offering insights into the island's rich heritage.

Adventure golf: Families can enjoy a fun-filled day at the adventure golf course located at Sandy Ground. The course features 18 holes with various obstacles and challenges, providing entertainment for both children and adults.

Romantic experiences for couples

Anguilla is a perfect destination for couples seeking a romantic getaway. With its stunning beaches, luxurious resorts, and intimate dining options, there are plenty of opportunities for couples to create lasting memories. Here are some romantic experiences to consider:

Private beaches: Anguilla boasts secluded and picturesque beaches that offer privacy and tranquility for couples. Rent a beachfront villa or book a resort with a private beach to enjoy romantic walks, sunset picnics, or simply bask in the beauty of the surroundings.

Sunset cruises: Embark on a romantic sunset cruise to witness the breathtaking beauty of Anguilla's coastline as the sun sets over the Caribbean Sea. Many tour operators offer private charters or group cruises with dinner and drinks included, providing the perfect setting for a romantic evening.

Couples' spa treatments: Indulge in a couples' spa treatment at one of Anguilla's luxurious spas. Enjoy a relaxing massage, a rejuvenating facial, or a romantic couples' package that includes a variety of treatments designed to enhance relaxation and intimacy.

Fine dining: Anguilla is home to numerous award-winning restaurants that offer intimate and romantic dining experiences. Enjoy candlelit dinners on the beach, rooftop dining with panoramic views, or private dining in secluded settings. Many restaurants specialize in fresh seafood and international cuisine, ensuring a memorable culinary experience.

Sunset horseback riding: Take a romantic horseback ride along the beach during sunset. Several equestrian centers in Anguilla offer guided rides for couples, allowing them to explore the island's natural beauty while enjoying moments of serenity and connection.

Childcare services and amenities for families

Anguilla understands the needs of families traveling with children and provides various childcare services and amenities. Here are some options available:

Resorts with kids' clubs: Many resorts in Anguilla offer kids' clubs or supervised activities for children. These clubs provide age-appropriate programs and entertainment, giving parents the opportunity to relax while their children engage in supervised play.

Babysitting services: Several resorts and hotels offer babysitting services upon request. Professional babysitters can be arranged to take care of children while parents enjoy some alone time or go out for a romantic dinner.

Family-friendly accommodations: Anguilla offers a range of family-friendly accommodations, including villas and resorts with spacious rooms or suites that can accommodate families. These accommodations often provide amenities such as cribs, high chairs, and childproofing options.

Outdoor playgrounds: Some resorts and public areas in Anguilla have outdoor playgrounds where children can safely play and interact with other kids. These playgrounds are equipped with age-appropriate equipment and provide a fun and safe environment for children to enjoy.

Kid-friendly restaurants: Many restaurants in Anguilla welcome families and offer kid-friendly menus or options. These restaurants often provide high chairs, booster seats, and a relaxed atmosphere suitable for families with children.

It's important to note that the availability of childcare services and amenities may vary depending on the specific resort or accommodation chosen. It's advisable to check with the chosen accommodation or tour operator in advance to ensure that suitable options are available for families traveling with children.

Chapter Ten: Day Trips and Excursions from Anguilla

Nearby islands and their attractions (St. Martin, St. Barths, etc.)

Anguilla's location in the Caribbean makes it an ideal base for day trips and excursions to nearby islands. Here are some nearby islands and their attractions that are worth exploring:

St. Martin: Just a short ferry ride away from Anguilla, St. Martin offers a different cultural experience with its blend of French and Dutch influences. Visitors can explore the charming streets of Marigot, the capital of the French side, and enjoy shopping for local crafts and souvenirs. The island is also known for its beautiful beaches, such as Orient Bay and Maho Beach, where visitors can witness planes landing just a few meters above their heads.

St. Barths: Another popular day trip destination from Anguilla is St. Barths, a luxurious island known for its upscale resorts, designer boutiques, and gourmet dining options. Visitors can spend the day exploring the picturesque capital of Gustavia, with its colorful buildings and yacht-filled harbor.

St. Barths also boasts stunning beaches, including Shell Beach and Colombier Beach, which can be reached by boat or hiking.

Prickly Pear Cays: Located just off the coast of Anguilla, the Prickly Pear Cays are a group of uninhabited islands that offer a pristine natural environment for snorkeling and beachcombing. Visitors can take a boat tour to these cays and enjoy crystal-clear waters, vibrant coral reefs, and white sandy beaches. The cays are also home to diverse marine life, making them a popular spot for snorkeling enthusiasts.

Scrub Island: Situated northeast of Anguilla, Scrub Island is a small uninhabited island that is perfect for a day trip adventure. Visitors can take a boat tour to the island and explore its untouched beaches, hike through scenic trails, or snorkel in the surrounding coral reefs. Scrub Island offers a peaceful and secluded getaway, allowing visitors to connect with nature and enjoy the unspoiled beauty of the Caribbean.

Guided tours and excursions to neighboring destinations

There are several guided tours and excursions available from Anguilla that allow visitors to explore neighboring destinations. These tours provide convenience, expert guidance, and the opportunity to learn about the history, culture, and natural beauty of the region. Here are some popular guided tours and excursions:

Island hopping tours: Many tour operators offer island hopping tours that allow visitors to explore multiple nearby islands in a single day. These tours often include stops at St. Martin, St. Barths, and other nearby islands, providing a comprehensive experience of the region's diverse culture and attractions.

Snorkeling and diving tours: Anguilla is surrounded by pristine coral reefs, making it a paradise for snorkeling and diving enthusiasts. Guided snorkeling and diving tours are available, taking visitors to the best spots to explore underwater ecosystems teeming with colorful fish, coral formations, and other marine life.

Historical and cultural tours: Anguilla has a rich history and vibrant culture that can be explored through guided tours. These tours often include visits to historical sites such as the Wallblake House, the oldest surviving plantation house on the island, and the Heritage Collection Museum, which showcases artifacts related to Anguilla's history.

Visitors can also learn about the island's African heritage and colonial past through guided tours.

Boat tours and charters: Boat tours and charters are popular in Anguilla, offering visitors the opportunity to explore the coastline, visit secluded beaches, and discover hidden coves. These tours often include stops for snorkeling, swimming, and beach picnics, providing a memorable experience of Anguilla's natural beauty.

Recommendations for day trips exploring Anguilla's surroundings:

While Anguilla itself offers a wealth of attractions and activities, there are also several day trips within the island's vicinity that allow visitors to explore its surroundings. Here are some recommendations for day trips from Anguilla:

Sandy Island: Located just off the coast of Sandy Ground, Sandy Island is a small uninhabited islet that can be reached by boat. Visitors can spend the day on this idyllic island, enjoying pristine beaches, snorkeling in clear waters, and feasting on fresh seafood at the island's restaurant.

Little Bay: Accessible only by boat or by swimming from Crocus Bay, Little Bay is a secluded beach surrounded by cliffs and crystal-clear waters. Visitors can take a boat tour or rent kayaks to reach this hidden gem and spend the day swimming, snorkeling, and enjoying the peaceful atmosphere.

Scilly Cay: Situated off the coast of Island Harbour, Scilly Cay is a tiny island known for its rustic beach bar and restaurant. Visitors can take a short boat ride to the island and enjoy a delicious lunch or dinner of grilled lobster or crayfish, accompanied by live music and stunning views of the Caribbean Sea.

Pristine Cove: Located on the eastern side of Anguilla, Pristine Cove is a secluded beach known for its unspoiled beauty and tranquility. Visitors can take a short hike to reach this hidden gem and spend the day sunbathing, swimming, and enjoying the peaceful surroundings.

Katouche Cave: For those interested in exploring Anguilla's natural wonders, a visit to Katouche Cave is highly recommended. This limestone cave system offers a fascinating underground experience with stalactites, stalagmites, and underground pools. Guided tours are available to explore the cave's chambers and learn about its geological significance.

These day trips provide opportunities to discover the diverse landscapes, natural wonders, and cultural gems that surround Anguilla, enhancing the overall travel experience.

Chapter Eleven: Sustainable Tourism in Anguilla

Eco-friendly practices in Anguilla

Anguilla is committed to sustainable tourism practices and has implemented various initiatives to protect its natural environment and promote eco-friendly tourism. The island's government, along with local businesses and organizations, actively work towards preserving its pristine beaches, marine life, and natural resources. Here are some eco-friendly practices in Anguilla:

Renewable energy: Anguilla is increasingly investing in renewable energy sources, such as solar power, to reduce its reliance on fossil fuels. Many resorts and hotels have installed solar panels to generate electricity, contributing to a more sustainable energy system.

Waste management: The island has implemented waste management programs to minimize the impact of tourism on its environment. Recycling facilities are available throughout the island, and efforts are made to reduce single-use plastics. Visitors are encouraged to dispose of their waste responsibly and participate in recycling initiatives.

Water conservation: Anguilla faces water scarcity issues, particularly during dry seasons. To address this, hotels and resorts have implemented water conservation measures, such as installing low-flow showerheads and toilets, and collecting rainwater for irrigation purposes. Visitors are encouraged to be mindful of their water usage and support these conservation efforts.

Sustainable agriculture: Anguilla promotes sustainable agriculture practices, including organic farming and locally sourced produce. Many restaurants and resorts prioritize using locally grown ingredients and supporting local farmers, reducing the carbon footprint associated with food transportation.

Responsible tourism tips for visitors

As a responsible tourist, there are several actions you can take to support sustainable tourism practices in Anguilla. Here are some tips:

Respect the environment: When visiting beaches, nature reserves, or other natural areas, ensure you follow all rules and regulations. Do not litter, disturb wildlife, or damage coral reefs while snorkeling or diving. Leave only footprints behind and take your trash with you.

Conserve water: Anguilla experiences water scarcity issues, so be mindful of your water usage. Take shorter showers, turn off taps when not in use, and report any leaks or water wastage to the hotel staff.

Support nearby organizations: Pick privately claimed facilities, eateries, and visit administrators that focus on manageable practices and backing the nearby economy. By doing so, you contribute to the community's well-being and help preserve the island's culture.

Reduce plastic waste: Bring a reusable water bottle and refill it instead of purchasing single-use plastic bottles. Say no to plastic straws, bags, and other disposable items. Many establishments in Anguilla have already transitioned to eco-friendly alternatives, so support their efforts by choosing sustainable options.

Learn about the local culture and environment: Take the time to learn about Anguilla's history, culture, and natural environment. Engage with local communities, visit museums and cultural sites, and participate in educational tours that promote environmental awareness. This will deepen your understanding of the island's heritage and conservation efforts.

Conservation efforts and nature preservation initiatives

Anguilla is dedicated to preserving its natural resources and has implemented various conservation efforts and nature preservation initiatives. Here are some notable initiatives:

Marine Protected Areas (MPAs): Anguilla has established MPAs to protect its marine ecosystems and biodiversity. These areas restrict fishing and other activities that may harm coral reefs, seagrass beds, and marine wildlife. Visitors are encouraged to respect these protected areas and follow guidelines for responsible snorkeling, diving, and boating.

Sea Turtle Conservation: Anguilla is home to several species of sea turtles, including the critically endangered Hawksbill turtle. The Anguilla National Trust and other organizations work to protect nesting sites, monitor turtle populations, and raise awareness about the importance of conservation. Visitors can support these efforts by avoiding disturbing nesting sites and reporting any turtle sightings to local authorities.

Coastal Cleanup Initiatives: Regular beach cleanups are organized by local organizations and community groups to remove litter and debris from the island's shores. Visitors can participate in these cleanups or organize their own beach cleanup during their stay. This helps maintain the beauty of Anguilla's beaches and prevents marine pollution.

Environmental Education Programs: The Anguilla National Trust and other organizations offer environmental education programs for locals and visitors alike. These programs aim to raise awareness about the island's unique ecosystems, conservation challenges, and sustainable practices. Visitors can attend workshops, guided nature walks, or educational events to learn more about Anguilla's environment and contribute to its preservation.

By supporting these conservation efforts and practicing responsible tourism, visitors can help protect Anguilla's natural beauty for future generations to enjoy.

Conclusion

In conclusion, a tourist journey to Anguilla Island promises an unforgettable experience filled with natural beauty, sustainable practices, and a deep connection with the local community. From the moment you arrive on the island, you will be greeted by pristine beaches, crystal-clear waters, and a sense of tranquility that sets the stage for a truly rejuvenating vacation.

As you explore Anguilla, you will discover a destination that is committed to sustainability and eco-friendly practices. The use of renewable energy sources, waste management initiatives, water conservation measures, and sustainable agriculture practices all contribute to the preservation of the island's natural environment. By supporting these efforts and being a responsible tourist, you can actively contribute to the preservation of Anguilla's beauty.

During your stay, take the time to immerse yourself in the local culture and environment. Engage with the community by supporting local businesses, learning about their traditions, and participating in conservation initiatives. By reducing plastic waste, conserving water, and respecting the environment, you can make a positive impact on Anguilla's sustainability efforts.

Anguilla also offers numerous opportunities to engage in conservation efforts and nature preservation initiatives. Whether it's joining a marine protected area program, assisting in sea turtle conservation programs, participating in coastal cleanup initiatives, or taking part in environmental education programs, you can actively contribute to the protection of Anguilla's unique ecosystems and biodiversity.

Beyond its natural beauty and sustainability practices, Anguilla provides a chance to connect with a community that values its natural resources and is dedicated to preserving them for future generations. By embracing responsible tourism and supporting the island's conservation efforts, you are ensuring that Anguilla's splendor will continue to captivate visitors for years to come.

In summary, a journey to Anguilla Island offers more than just a luxurious beach getaway. It provides an opportunity to experience a destination that prioritizes sustainability, engages with its community, and values its natural resources. By being a responsible tourist and actively supporting the island's conservation initiatives, you can contribute to the preservation of Anguilla's natural beauty and create lasting memories of a truly remarkable travel experience.

Made in the USA
Middletown, DE
01 November 2023

41780794R00049